EMPOWERING HOPE

EMPOWERING HOPE

THOUGHTS TO BRIGHTEN YOUR DAY

JOSEPH G. DONDERS

TWENTY-THIRD PUBLICATIONS
Mystic, Connecticut

Acknowledgments

Thanks for all those who cooperated in the preparation of this book: Ms. Grace Muite of the Kenya Catholic Secretariat in Nairobi who commissioned most of the texts for her program *Lift Up Your Heart* of the Voice of Kenya; Ms. Rosemary Barwa, secretary at St. Paul's University Chaplaincy in Nairobi; Sr. Mary Godfrey who did the final editing of the manuscript; and the staff at Twenty-Third Publications who directed the final production.

Most of the texts were used in radio broadcasts in Kenya, Africa, some in the United States in the television program *From Real to Reel*. The texts were written to be spoken aloud. You might read them to others . . . but read them first yourself!

Twenty-Third Publications
P.O. Box 180
Mystic, CT 06355
(203) 536-2611

Library of Congress Catalog Card Number 85-51480
ISBN 0-89622-281-0

CONTENTS

Empowering Hope

There was a father who for nearly half an hour had been listening quietly to his son. Because the father didn't often have time to listen to his son, the boy was enjoying this special occasion. Profiting by the listening mood of his father, the son described at length what he was planning to do with his life and especially what he hoped he could help to do about some of the problems in the world.

He talked enthusiastically about his ideals of justice and integrity, goodness and fairness, about a new world order, and things like that. The father listened until the boy's long monologue came to an end. Then he said, "Wait until you're a bit older, son. Wait until you have tasted a bit more of life, and all that will blow over."

What a pity the father had to say that. But how often do we respond to the enthusiasms of the young with some remark very similar. So many parents, so many teachers, so many lecturers, so many professionals respond in the same way to the optimistic expectations of our boys and girls, young men and young women who come to us with their enthusiasm and their brilliant eyes full of hope. We say, "When you are older, you will become more realistic! Wait and see!"

We tell them to be realistic. We imply that their expectations are unrealistic, misplaced, and stupid. Our remarks even imply that to be young is unwise.

It is all very sad. I think that it is one of the reasons why there is so much frustration in our schools, colleges, and universities. That is why it must be so encouraging for our youth to meet an older person who is still hopeful, who is not disillusioned and bitter, a person who has become more realistic through the experience of life but who has not lost hope or enthusiasm.

Jesus was like that during his days upon the earth. He spoke about the seed of divinity and goodness that would grow through all difficulties to become a great tree where everyone could find a home.

His disciple, Saint Paul, was like that, too. When Paul had to write that Demas had left him "because he loved the world," that Alexander the coppersmith had caused him a great deal of harm, and that all the others had forsaken him, he nevertheless did not give up hope. He did not turn bitter. He did not become what some would call a "realist."

Paul also recorded that Crescens had gone on mission to Galatia, Titus to Dalmatia, and Tychicus to Ephesus to preach the gospel. That was his hope: the seed of God was going to be sown. The gospel was going to be spread around the world (2 Timothy 4).

Let this be a lesson. Don't crush the hope in our children! If you do, you are saying there is no hope. And how can we be called believers without hope?

The Day After

Have you ever awakened early in the morning with a vague feeling that something went wrong the day before? At first you don't remember what it was. But then, suddenly, it comes back to you. Just before going to bed that night, you had a quarrel with your partner, with your son, with your father, or with your mother. You were angry and upset, and you suddenly said, "I am going to bed!" and you slammed the door behind you. Then, just before you fell asleep, you heard the door slam again. The one you had difficulties with went to bed also. Things like this don't happen every day, but they do happen.

The next morning, you come out of your bed and the memory of last night comes back. You gnash your teeth and clench your fists and prepare for the battle.

There is only one way to overcome that difficulty, really. It is a way, according to the Son of God that is given to each of us. Do you remember how Jesus one evening breathed upon his apostles and said to them: "Receive the Holy Spirit. I give you the power to forgive one another."

You can do it. We can do it. We can forgive one another. Not only can we do it, we should do it. If we do not forgive one another, we will not be able to live together. We do not have to dramatize our forgiveness. We do not have to do it solemnly; we do not have to do it in writing. We can do it very simply, by a pat on the shoulder, by a "good morning." By asking, "Would you like a cup of tea?" Let us do it. Let us clear the atmosphere. Let us use the powers given us by our Savior.

Prayer for Peace

There is one prayer that most of you may have heard. It has been handed out by the thousands of copies in this country. You find it everywhere—in shops, restaurants, libraries, homes, offices. You might find it on a secretary's desk or on the wall above her head competing with some other nugget of wisdom, such as "The Boss Is Always Boss," and the like. It is a prayer that has given consolation to millions. It is a prayer that can be said by all because it is interdenominational. It was most probably written about seven hundred years ago by Saint Francis of Assisi:

> Lord, make me an instrument of your peace.
> Where there is hatred, let me sow love;
> Where there is doubt, faith;
> Where there is despair, hope;
> Where there is darkness, light;
> And where there is sadness, joy.

O divine Master, grant that I may not so much seek
To be consoled, as to console;
To be understood, as to understand;
To be loved, as to love;
For it is in giving that we receive;
It is pardoning that we are pardoned;
And it is in dying that we are born to eternal life.

Francis did not merely compose that beautiful prayer and occasionally recite it. He lived it. He lived it in a most radical way. Just imagine that all of us, here in our country, our city, our place of work, our home, would pray that prayer sincerely and with all our heart. It might change our world if so many hearts were "lifted up." Lord, make us an instrument of your peace.

Holding It All Together

Did you ever hear the story about the little bird who wouldn't fly? There was this small bird lying on his back with his legs in the air. He had an anxious look on his face. You could read the worry in his round black eyes. Now and then he sighed, and you could overhear him repeating to himself: "You must go on. It is your vocation! It is your responsibility! Be brave! Everything depends on it!"

Another bird passed, high in the sky. Looking down, he saw his little brother lying on his back. Thinking there might have been some mishap, he came down to have a better look. "Are you ill?" he asked. The answer was, "No." "Are you unwell?" Again the answer was, "No." "Is there something wrong with you?" Again, "No." "Then what are you doing on your back? Why aren't you flying about, free as a bird?" The fellow on his back sighed very deeply and said, "Don't you see that I am holding up the sky with my feet? If I should turn over, the sky would fall down and then even you would not be able to fly around any more. I bear the responsibility for the whole of the universe!"

Just at that moment there was a gust of wind. Not very strong, just a breath, but enough to detach a leaf from a tree above. The bird did not see it until it fell just behind his head. Startled and frightened, the little bird scrambled to his feet and flew off. The sky remained in its place.

Prophets have told us that we overburden ourselves with all kinds of things. Jesus said so, too. He said that we should rid ourselves of false burdens, stupid pretenses. He said that we should not be so richly laden, that we should be humble and prudent. He advised us not to worry too much about tomorrow. He told us to be at peace with our brothers and sisters. He asked us to share with others and give them freedom to grow. Let's do that, and all of us will be happier.

Monday Morning Blues

I don't know how you feel, but I don't always feel fine on a Monday morning. Do you wake up and start to think about the things you are supposed to do—at home and at work? Then there are those other problems: the stories you overheard someone saying about you; the quarrel you had with one of your co-workers, or worse, with one of the members of your family. Besides all that, there is the continual lack of money. Just yesterday your child informed you that her teacher told her she should have new gym shoes, or another textbook, and who knows what else.

It is very difficult to remain serene and pleasant under those circumstances. It is difficult to keep smiling and greeting people and saying that everything is going well. But listen, all this is true not only of you, but of almost everybody. If I am right in thinking that you feel depressed this morning, moody, and irritated, then you are not alone.

If the people sitting next to you on the bus or standing almost on top of you in the elevator are silent so early on Monday morning, it is because they don't feel too happy either. Those thousands and thousands who are driving to work, who are going to their shops, who are opening the doors of their offices, or beginning their tasks at home most probably feel a bit like you and me. I don't say they are basically unhappy, but they are probably not too light-hearted either.

If we make ourselves aware of this, if we take it into account when we come into contact with others, we can more ably live together as brothers and sisters. If we don't try, we will miss the chance that the present moment gives us, and we may regret it afterward.

So this morning, before listening to the news, before you finish your cup of coffee or tea, and before you leave the house, ask God to be with you and with all the others you are going to meet this day, and all will be well.

Showing Appreciation

We can learn from our experience with people. We can learn how to make others feel really good. Consider how others make you feel good. They call you by your name. They express their appreciation. They thank you for a kindness or a service. And you feel elated and happy and capable of doing more. Everyone who thinks about it for a moment knows this.

I know a parish priest who was famous among his colleagues for his ability to raise funds for his parish activities. His colleagues, who were less than succesful in the same enterprise, were a bit jealous. Every Sunday they talked money to their parishioners. They went so far as to pound the pulpit, to shout at the congregation, even throwing back in anger the nickles and the dimes of the collection. They quoted the Bible in support of contribution to the work of the Lord. They spoke about ingratitude, and I don't know what else, but with little success. Each Sunday they were faced with paying parish expenses with the small change of the collection while their neighboring pastor counted the bank notes and made plans for new parish services.

His colleagues decided to send a spy to find out the secret of his success. The informer went several times to the church of the fundraiser and sat at the back of the church to listen. He waited for bursts of thunder and lightning, for threats and menaces, but he heard nothing of the kind. The only thing he noticed was that the preacher thanked the faithful each Sunday for their generous contribution of the Sunday before, and he praised them for their understanding and generosity. And stimulated by his gratitude and appreciation, his parishioners gave and gave and gave. He made them feel that their sacrifice was appreciated; he made them feel good.

Did you never notice how Jesus often used the same technique? Not to raise money; he never seemed interested in that kind of activity. Jesus used that technique with another end in view. Did you notice how he treated Zaccheus, a man who was despised by his countrymen as a tax-collector for the Romans and who perhaps despised himself? Jesus called Zaccheus "a true son of Abraham." Did you notice how he praised Mary Magdalen for the good he saw in her? Jesus made the people around him grow, not by pretending that they were what they were not, not by lying, but by appreciating in each of them their individual qualities, their real merit, their genuine good. He recognized in them the work and the hand of his Father in heaven. Let's express our appreciation for those around us today.

Dependence

Did you ever hear the story about the spider who weaved the most magnificent web? Long ago there was this spider, the kind that could weave beautiful gossamer webs. The spider, above all creatures, knows what "depending" means. His whole life depends on the fragile threads that constitute his home.

   This particular spider had made a beautiful web, a real piece of technical know-how and artistic insight, the absolute ideal combination, a really well-developed pattern. The web was so cleverly constructed that spiders from the neighborhood came to have a look at it. The web was so artistic, so symmetrical, that if you could have folded it over the middle thread, the two sides would have fitted exactly over each other. It was a real marvel. Unwary flies and mosquitos galore, whose curiosity drove them to take a closer look, were easily caught in the web.

Schools even started to organize trips to show their students this model web. The spider himself was very content with his creation. Late in the evening you could observe him sitting at the top of his creation, rubbing his tiny hind legs with great satisfaction.

One morning the spider decided to check his web once more. You never know, one or another adjustment or improvement might still be possible. No spider is infallible. He made the circuit of his web, strengthening a knot here, undoing another there. All seemed to be in order. Then he suddenly saw a thread he did not recognize. It definitely had not been spun by himself. It looked out of place. What could it be? A bit irritated and slightly over courageous, the spider went to examine the thread that seemed superfluous.

He looked along the length of the thread to see where it had come from or where it led. The thread was very long, disappearing from sight in the sky. The spider checked once more, then decided, without further hesitation, to bite through the useless thread.

It broke. Suddenly it was as if the whole world of that spider came down. The beautiful web collapsed like a soap bubble in cold water. The thread on which the spider's whole world depended had been disconnected. What a fall the spider had!

Sometimes you hear people say, "I don't believe in that God story any more!" Or they seem to be so successful in life that they forget about God totally. They do not realize that the whole meaning of life depends on that relationship, that connection with God. They cut the thread. They make a mistake. They are hanging in mid air, and what a fall they will have if they do not reconnect themselves in time. Who are we without that thread?

Scapegoat

Let us hope and pray that everything will go well today. But if something goes wrong, I am sure that it will not be your fault! At least that may be what you will say.

When something goes wrong, we always find a culprit. It is always someone else. It is never our fault. It is never my fault. It is never your fault either. And because everyone has that same tendency of blaming others, then no one is guilty of anything at all. You just start wondering why things happen as they do.

It has been that way from the very beginning. Do you remember when God asked Adam, "What did you do?" Adam answered, "It was not me; it was Eve." And Eve said, "It was not me; it was the snake!" and the snake crept away. As long as we "pass the buck" of our responsibility to others, this world is never going to change, at least as far as our part in it is concerned.

There is a story about an example of this rule. It was told years ago by a Japanese preacher. There was in Japan a university in serious difficulties. The students were on strike. They threw stones at passing cars. They uprooted signposts. They barricaded the roads. The situation was one big, chaotic mess. The police did not know what to do, and the lecturers did not dare to move through the campus anymore.

Suddenly, the main door of the university opened. Out came the chancellor. Without showing any fear, he walked straight up to the students on the main campus. He climbed on a table and began to speak. At first no one could hear or understand what he was saying, but then the nearest ones started to shout for silence. Silence, though with difficulty, finally fell.

The chancellor addressed them: "Comrades, our university is in chaos. Things are not going well at all. Somebody must be at fault." At that point of his speech, he produced a thin bamboo rod from his pocket and began to beat himself on his left hand until the blood flowed.

The students at first looked on in silence. They could not understand what was happening. Then they began to protest. They shouted that he should stop, that he was not the only one at fault, nor the worst one. They shouted that they wanted to talk.

The Japanese preacher who told the story was making an analogy between his story and the story of Jesus. He wanted to say that Jesus had taken all our sins upon himself (1 Corinthians 15:3).

I think the analogy goes a bit far. But we can definitely learn from this story that as long as we absolve ourselves of al blame and accuse others for the chaos in this world, nothing will change. And that would be a great pity because then we would be contributing to that chaos instead. Would we not? Let us change.

A Pack Animal

Life is not easy. You can see it in the way people walk to their work, in the way they queue up for their bus, in the way they do not greet each other. You can see it in the listless way the children often carry their bags of books to school.

People seem to walk and move as if they were carrying a heavy load. And many of us are! Maybe you, too. Some of that burden is unavoidable. If you have children, then there is the anxiety of school fees and school clothes and shoes. If you are a student, you have to carry the burden of assignments, papers, tests, and final exams. If you are a student with a family and a child to care for, they may provide an extra burden.

But alongside all these unavoidable, necessary, and often unpleasant burdens, too many of us carry an unnecessary extra load. Some of us are like pack animals with their freight hanging all around them. We might be burdening ourselves with too many possessions. We might own so many things that anxiety about them immobilizes us. We might cling to all kinds of useless things that can burden us. We might be burdened by guilt or wrong doing that we should have talked about with someone long ago. But for some reason we did not want to do that. We kept silent.

We might be burdened with the memory of an old injury. Someone grievously offended us years ago and we could not forgive, we could not forget. We might be burdened by an illicit, improper, or unjust relationship that we should have ended long ago. But we didn't. Instead, we fostered that harmful relationship.

That is why so many of us are so heavy-laden as we move through our days, unable really to enjoy the passing days, bound up and unfree.

Jesus said that anyone who carries too heavy a burden will not be able to pass through the narrow gate leading to life. He used the comparison of a rich-laden camel, so freighted with expensive merchandise that it could not pass through the gate leading into town.

Would it not be possible for you to unload yourself somewhat today? Speak with someone about your problem. Forgive another. Break that strange relationship. Free yourself and breathe. Throw off that load and walk!

Contemplating Suicide

Some time ago I received a letter from a far-off country. The person who wrote to me was, I think, a student. I'm not sure because I never met him. I don't even know how he got my name.

The writer confided to me that he was contemplating suicide. He asked me whether I could give him a good reason why he should not carry out his intent. He described for me the logical steps in his reasoning that had brought him to this point. This is how he expressed it:

> The Creator has always been described to me as almighty, so he could help me in my difficulties either by ordinary means or by a miracle. I know that man is a dual being and that sickness and pain live only in the mortal clay-body. If, then, I cut short my clay-body life on earth, if I shake off the clay-body, then the spiritual

body will be liberated to move freely and happily to a better place of existence where there is no suffering.

If I, the sufferer, do this to help myself, why should the Creator, a non co-sufferer, blame me, a poor, finite entity?

The writer ended up by saying that perhaps his reasoning was immature and faulty. I think he is not the only one who sometimes reasons like that. Perhaps you sympathize with him. That is why I'll tell you how I answered his letter:

Dear Friend,

I think that there are quite a number of reasons why you should not shake off what you call your clay-body. It is as if you are living and reasoning in "splendid isolation." Did you ever consider that you should see your life not only as a gift from God to you, but also as a gift from God to others?

If you disappear from this world, are you not going to increase the sufferings of those to whom you are related by blood or other bonds? Have they not, in a sense, the right to your friendship, your love, your attention, your service? The South African (or if you prefer) the Azanian theologian, Manasse Buthelezi, stresses this point very much. He writes that we must consider ourselves as gifts from God to others, and others as gifts from God to us.

I don't know whether you agree with what I wrote. My unknown correspondent agreed. He wrote me that he had never thought along those lines. He wrote that the thought had given him a purpose, a task in life. He said that he would never look upon himself again as isolated or alone. Let us not do that either.

Evil Spirits

You say you don't believe in evil spirits? I do. I will tell you why. I heard the case of a boy who had an old bike. He brought it to a bike shop to have a ten-speed gear shift put in. When he went to pick up the bike, he found that he would have to pay 200 dollars for the repairs. The boy did not have the money; he had never dreamed that it would cost so much. The repairman saw his hesitation and said sharply, "If you don't come with the money before the end of the month, I will sell your bike for my costs."

The boy returned home and tried everywhere to obtain the money. No one was willing to give such a sum. It was too much. The boy was desperate. Then one day the door of a house in the neighborhood was left open. The boy asked some people around whether there was anybody in the house. They said, "No." Seeing an opportunity when no one was in sight, the boy slipped into the house. When he came out with a radio cassette recorder, he was caught and apprehended.

Now he stood face to face with his captors. In tears, he protested over and over again, "Don't call me a thief! I am not a thief! I am not a thief!"

One of them remarked, "All right. you say you are not a thief. But who stole that radio?" The radio stood in front of him on a table. For a moment the boy was silent; then he said, looking at it: "The bicycle!"

What he said was not true. It was nonsense. But in a way, what he said was right. His bicycle had come so important to him that it overruled and overpowered every other consideration. He had become obsessed by it. His bike was like an evil spirit, dominating him.

He was only a child; but how many of us, older and supposedly wiser, are not obssessed as the boy was with the thought of something we want: a car, a promotion, a VCR, a house. If we are not careful, those justifiable desires can take over and control us completely. They can blind, paralyze, and deafen us. It is very necessary in our lives that we chase away those evil spirits. That is perhaps the reason why Jesus so often drove them away. So should we, with his help, drive them away from us and from around us, and our world will be happier.

You Are an Eagle

A man caught an eagle—that king among birds, proud and strong, large and beautiful. Since he didn't know what to do with it, he put it in a henhouse. At first the chickens were afraid, but then the hens and the cocks and even the small chicks got accustomed to their guest. The eagle, too, became used to his new surroundings, and even to the chicken food, since he had nothing else to eat.

Then one day a visitor came to the man's house. He saw the eagle in the henhouse surrounded by the hens and said, "That bird is an eagle! How long has it been cooped up in that henhouse? You should take it out and let it fly free. It is a crime for an eagle to be treated like a chicken!"

"But this one has become quite tame like the hens. It even cackles like a hen."

"Impossible," said the visitor. "You can't make a hen out of an eagle. Let me show you, may I?"

"Go ahead," his host said. "You will see that I am right. It has become a hen, a frightened chicken."

The visitor carefully opened the henhouse door, took out the huge bird, set it on his wrist, lifted it into the air and said, "You are an eagle. You belong in the sky and not on the ground. Go and fly!"

The eagle looked around, clucked like a frightened chicken but did not move. Then the man turned the eagle into the light of the rising sun. The eagle looked at the sun, then suddenly spread its enormous wings, cried exultantly like an eagle and flew higher and higher, never to return again.

You are the eagle living in the henhouse, hemmed in, fenced in by all kinds of small things: fame, honor, greed, career hunting, regulations, rites, and so on. You know that you are captive of all these things and not truly free. You know that you were born for another type of life.

The turning point in this story was when the man turned the bird into the light of the rising sun. It was the sun that made the bird free. You can fill in for yourself who that sun is. See the light!

Success Formula

Many people today are searching for a success formula in life. They read books on how to be influential and make friends, how to study, or how to become rich. You can find them at their books even during the early hours of morning; and the children are not allowed to play or make noise in the house because Mom or Dad is studying in view of a better future.

There is one thing all these seekers are sure of: If they could find some way to be "in tune with the forces of nature," if they could somehow enter the "mainstream of life," all would become easy. But where and how can one enter that stream where everything seems to succeed?

That was the question of Francis of Assisi seven centuries ago. He tried in all kinds of ways. He tried romance. He courted the most beautiful girls in town, and to win their favor, dressed magnificently. He played love ballads on his guitar and sang beneath their windows far into the night until the neighbors, annoyed, pelted him with shoes or whatever else came to hand.

He tried glory. He purchased expensive arms and a magnificent war-horse, and in the company of some of his young friends, marched off to war to the martial music of the local band. But the battle was lost. His enemies captured him and marched him ignominiously to prison.

He tried commerce. He began his apprenticeship with his father, one of the textile-barons in town. But he gave so much away to the poor and to his friends that his father, in anger, finally had him arrested. When Francis appeared before the court, he appealed to the bishop of the town. A date for the hearing was set, and Francis and his father appeared before the bishop for a verdict. The case was explained: Francis had taken goods without permission and sold them to give the money to the poor. The bishop gave his verdict: Francis must repay the money to his father.

Francis answered, "Gladly, and more." He disappeared behind a door and in a moment returned stark naked with his costly clothing in his hands. He handed his rich apparel to his father and with this gesture renounced forever his inheritance. "From now on," he said, "I have only one father, our Father, who art in heaven." The bishop was shocked by the scene and covered Francis with his cape to hide his nakedness. But Francis had found his way. He had found access to the only real power in the universe: God his Father.

Francis was free, unbound, and unmarried. We on our part have our jobs, our families, our many responsibilities. But we, too, can have access to the same power. We can be faithful and successful in our responsibilities and our relationships if we place our whole life in God's hands; if we, too, say "Our Father in Heaven."

Power and Giving

You have power; everyone of us has power. And sometimes we like to display it to others.

Once there was a country in which the king had died. The terrible thing was that some weeks before his only son, the crown prince, had died too. The crown prince had left twin sons behind. They were only six years old.

Parliament decided that the mother of the two would be queen until the moment when one of her two sons would assume the crown at age eighteen. But which one of the two? Even their mother did not remember which had been born first. They resembled each other too closely. So Parliament decided to appoint a committee of wise men to study the behavior of the two.

After close observation, it seemed to the committee that both young princes were equally fit for the task. But they could have only one king! And so they decided to ask the wisest person in the country to decide for them. That wisest person was an old woman living far from town in a forest. She said she would like to observe the two princes during their sleep.

That night she very carefully entered the room of the young sleeping princes. She studied them and noticed that there was a difference. One slept with his hands relaxed and open while the other slept with his fists tightly closed. She reported her findings to Parliament to make a decision. They did. The members decided to choose the open-handed prince as their future king.

This is, of course, only a fairy tale. But like all fairy tales, it reveals one of the deepest desires of humanity. We would like to meet people who use their power with open-handed generosity towards others.

Some days ago I needed a form. You need very many forms these days. I went to the man in charge of distributing them. He had them, I was sure. I could see them in the drawer of the desk he had left open. I asked for the form. He said, "I am sorry, but I have none at the moment. Can you come back tomorrow?"

Why did he say that? Was it to glory in the petty power he had over me? Was it because he derived some small satisfaction from another's inconvenience?

I went back the next day. He gave me the form from the pile I had seen the day before. I think that man had slept with his fists closed all during his youth.

It is said somewhere, "Give, and it shall be given to you. Give with full measure, and full measure shall be returned to you. Give with a joyful heart, and your days will be filled with joy." You cannot give with a closed fist, neither can you receive with a closed fist.

Moment to Moment

There was a man very experienced in meditation and prayer. He was asked how he could be so meditative, notwithstanding his strenuous professional life. He answered:

> When I stand, I stand; when I go, I go;
> when I sit, I sit; when I speak, I speak;
> and when I eat, I eat.

The person who interviewed him said, "All right. That is what all of us do. What else do you do?" And again he answered

> When I stand, I stand; when I go, I go;
> when I sit, I sit; when I speak, I speak;
> and when I eat, I eat.

And again the other said, "But that is what we do, too." And then he said:

That is not true. When you stand,
you are already thinking about sitting. When you
go, you are already thinking about arriving. When
you speak, you are already thinking about the
things you are going to do. And when you eat, you
are already ready to leave!

That wise man was right about many of us. We never pay attention to what we are really doing. We never do the things we are really busy with. All that we do, we do half-heartedly. This is a great pity. We always seem to be in a hurry. We always seem to be outside ourselves. We are thinking more about the next move than about the present move. We are working more at our promotion than at our work. And when we live like that, we are never fully alive!

On one occasion I met a middle-aged man who had been studying for most of his life. He had never really settled down; he was always on the move. He came to see me. I asked him what I could do for him. He answered, "I would like to continue my studies." I said, "But you already have two degrees!" That was true, but he said, "I do not feel qualified as yet." I asked him, "How old are you?" He said, "That doesn't matter, does it?" I knew he was over forty. I know that he will be studying for something he will never do.

Let us be attentive to our lives. Let us do well what we have to do and what we are engaged in doing. A teacher who is thinking only about climbing the professional ladder does not teach well. The clerk who is only thinking about promotion is most probably neglecting his job. Of course, we should improve and make progress in life. But we should live, too.

Is that why Jesus said, "Do not worry about tomorrow, tomorrow will take care of itself. Let the day's own trouble be sufficient for the day." I think that is right. When you stand, stand; when you go, go; when you sit, sit; when you speak, speak; when you eat, eat. Then you will live, and all will be well, from moment to moment.

Greetings Are Blessings (1)

She had come to town to begin her studies. She had never been in town before, having always lived upcountry in Africa. When I met her, she had gotten over her first surprise and astonishment. She told me that it was her first visit, and I asked her what struck her most.

I expected her to speak about the traffic, the high buildings, the variety of goods in the shops, or the crowds representing such a colorful variety of people. She looked around and said, "People do not greet each other in town." I was amazed by her answer. "Is that what struck you most?" "Yes," she answered, "Where I live, we always greet each other, but here no one greets anyone."

I looked around; it was true. People were passing each other at high speed; they avoided looking at the persons they passed, almost as if they were afraid, and they did not speak with each other at all. Mind you, we were not at the train station or a shopping mall. We were standing on the main campus of the university with scores of students milling around.

A day or two before this, I had been browsing in the campus library. I had found a book entitled *Antique Chinese Wisdom*. I had been struck by the great antiquity of some of these texts. One riddle I read was "Which is the best of these three: a teaching, a story, or a greeting?" The answer was "The best one is a greeting." Why?

I think it is because a greeting from another is like music to the ears, much more than a teaching or a story. To greet is to bless. To bless is to greet. If I greet you, I hope that you are going to speak in return. If you greet me, you expect me to respond. To greet means hoping that people will be open to one another, that they will reveal something of themselves. To greet means to respect another at the deepest level. To be greeted means to experience respect from another at the deepest level. To greet and to be greeted has something to do with eternity, with God in us, with God in you. Greetings to you.

Greetings Are Blessings (2)

It's been a very long time since the first day I went to town with my father. To a real town, I mean. We lived in a place we called a town, too, but it was more like an over-grown village.

I remember that first visit. The buildings were high, and when I looked at their tops, I got a crick in my neck. The traffic was hectic. I only dared to cross the street when I had my hand tightly in my father's. Those were not the strangest things I experienced. The strangest came at the moment I climbed down from the train that brought us to town. I began at once to do what I always did at home in my village. I began to greet the people we met as we walked along.

But the people stared at me with big eyes and did not return my greeting at all. Then I noticed that nobody greeted any one. They all passed each other without speaking, just like that. I looked at my father, who always greeted everybody he met in the street. He was not greeting anyone either, and he shook his head at me. He said, "Stop greeting!"

We, of course, greet one another. We shake hands left, right, and center. And because we do it so often, we get so accustomed to it, we forget how important a greeting is. As I wrote before, a greeting is a blessing.

You can realize that especially if someone refuses to greet you. Did that ever happen to you? You are in company together with others at a party or before a meeting. You greet one another. You shake hands. And then you put out your hand to greet an old friend or colleague, and he doesn't take your hand. There you are, standing with your hand in mid-air, dangling between heaven and earth. You don't know what to do. The others see what is happening to you, and you feel embarrassed. It is not only that. You know and you feel that the one who refuses to greet you wants to tell you, "I am not glad to see you! I don't enjoy your company! As far as I am concerned, I wish you were not here at all! As far as I am concerned, you might just as well fall dead!"

If you refuse to greet someone, you are in fact cursing him. Every greeting is a blessing. Every refusal to greet is a curse. Have you ever entered an office and had the official at the desk simply not look up when you said, "Good morning"? Didn't you feel upset, embarrassed after that, not knowing whether you should sit down or stand up? Have you ever been the one who refused to greet others? If you were, your refusal was like a curse, the greeting of a demon.

When Jesus met his disciples after his resurrection, he always greeted them, sometimes even twice. He said to them, "Peace be with you!" And he *looked* at them, and their hearts were lifted up. They felt warm inside, glorious, and victorious. He greeted *them*!

Saint Paul writes so often in his letters, "Please greet each other!" Saint Peter does the same. If you meet one another today, greet each one. Greet the ones you walk with, the ones you work with, the ones you travel with, the ones you live with. Greet one another, and God will be with you.

34

Consulting the Stars

There are days when everything seems to go wrong. You step out of your bed and trip over your shoe. You can't find your soap and your washbasin is clogged. There is no sugar for your coffee, then the bus is so crowded that you have to wait for the next one. You are late for work; and by ten o'clock you have gotten into a terrible row.

Everyone has days like that. Some people react by saying, "I shouldn't have gotten out of bed today, or I should have consulted my horoscope; I should have consulted my stars." Others put a note on their door, "Don't knock, nothing works today!" Some tell their colleagues or the members of the family at home, "Don't talk to me today, please." Others don't even go to work; they stay home and try to sleep or drink their ill luck away.

All this sounds a bit, or perhaps very primitive. It means that you think that your life is ruled by powers outside you.

That you have no control. That something else, or someone else, is controlling you. You say this yourself when you tell your friends, "This is not my day!" It is not your day. It is someone else's day, and that is why you tripped over that shoe, and did not find your soap, and had your washbasin clogged, and missed your bus, and developed a quarrel.

Would it be possible to turn the tide? Could you not start afresh? Are you not capable of taking the offensive, making a counter-move? Could you not find a few minutes in a silent corner, eyes closed, just for a split second, to put yourself into the hands of that superpower that rules the world and overcomes all evil? There is a power, the one out of whose hands you came, with whom who can overcome all evil in your life.

Saint Paul wrote about this ages ago, and he would repeat it for all those who, even today, look to their stars and their horoscopes, who visit soothsayers, and who try to determine their so-called good days and bad days—in short, making themselves slaves of things that are their gods.

Paul wrote:

> You pay special attention to certain days, months, seasons, and years. I am worried about you! Can it be that all my work for you has been for nothing? Now that you know God, or should I say, now that God knows you, how is it that you turn back to those weak and pitiful ruling spirits? Why do you want to become their slaves all over again? (Galatians 4:8-12).

Get into the counter-attack! Get into the offensive! Take your fate in your own hands by recommending yourself for a moment into the hand of almighty God for whom "all days are the same." Take courage, free yourself from stars and whatever binds you. Lift up your heart!

Going Nowhere

I want to tell you about an experience I had long ago. I tell it because I think you may have had an experience somewhat similar.

One of my uncles had come to visit our family. It was on a Sunday. He rode up on his motorbike, not a big one, more like a bike than a motorcycle. He put his motorbike very carefully into a shed behind the house because he was very proud of it. Then he came inside for a cup of tea and a visit to bring my parents up to date on family news.

I went outside with my brother, and, of course, just as you would have done, went straight to the shed to have a look at the motorbike. At first we only looked at it. We did not dare to touch it. Then we grew a little bolder and extended a tentative finger toward the rear light, then the mudguard. We discussed with each other how we thought the motorbike worked, though neither of us knew.

We started to push buttons and a light flashed on and off. We moved the pedals as we pushed buttons and suddenly, totally unexpectedly, the motorbike started to purr, prr, prr, prr . . . . We were alarmed and scared, but nobody in the house seemed to hear us. Then my brother shouted, "They're coming!" And yes, there in the doorway my uncle was standing with my father and my mother, talking away.

"Switch it off!" I screamed at my brother. "But how?" he answered, pushing buttons and gripping the handles. We could not stop it. The only thing we dared do was to run away. You can guess the rest of the story.

Did you ever have an experience like that one? When you switched something on that you could not switch off? When you started to run down a hill so fast that you could not stop? I think that many of us have had such an experience perhaps more than once during our lives.

Once a monk came for a visit in the house where some of us lived. We were extremely busy at the time (at least we thought so) and hardly had any time to greet the visitor upon his arrival. Later when one of us felt he had a little free time, he went for a brief talk. The monk took his hand, looked into his eyes, and smiled. "Let me tell you a story," he said. "There was a man in a car driving very fast over a road. An old farmer standing in the field saw him passing and shouted, 'Hey, driver, where are you going?' The driver had just the time to turn his head and answer, 'Don't ask me, ask my car!'"

The monk looked at him and continued, "That is how too many of you are. You are no longer masters of your own destiny. You have lost control over the powers that drive you. You are in motion, but you cannot stop to think it over."

Do you remember what Jesus told his disciples when they were all excited about his miracles and about themselves? "Let us go away from here, let us take a rest, let us pray a bit, let us come to ourselves!" We, too, need those moments, don't we? Take some of those moments for yourself today. If you do, your heart will be lifted up, and you might recapture your sense of direction.

Seeing God

Some days ago I heard a rather strange story. Two people were having a discussion. They were comparing the present with the past. They were not arguing that the past was better, but just that in the past, things were different from all points of view.

"There is one thing, however." said one. "In the past, people were much more religious. When I think of my father and my mother, my uncles and my aunts, I remember that whenever something happened to them, they always thought of God."

"But if you go back further," said the other, "you find more than that. Don't you remember how in former times, human beings sometimes saw God face to face? Think of Moses. Think of the prophets. Think of John."

At that moment, an old man passed them. He passed by when the two were looking at each other, silenced by their own question. He greeted them and asked, "Why do you look so worried?" One of the two friends said, "We are asking ourselves why in the old days people saw God face to face, and now nobody ever seems to see him."

The old man sat down beside them. "Do you really want to know?" They nodded, "Yes, do you know why?" "I think I do," he answered. "It is because today nobody wants to bend down."

"What do you mean?" the two asked almost simultaneously. For a moment he did not answer. Then the old man said, "It is because today nobody has time." The two sat in puzzled silence until he asked, "Do you understand what I said?" They shook their heads. He continued, "You can only find God near you, around you. God shows himself in your children if you take the time to look lovingly at them, if you bend down to them, forgetting all your worries. He shows himself in the rain, in the sun, in the animals, in the plants, in yourself. But today we seem to have no time. We are looking away from him. No wonder we do not see him any more."

The old man was right. When we are looking for God, we are often looking in the wrong direction. We are looking up, forgetting that the angels of God told the disciples who were gazing up into the sky where Jesus had disappeared, "You people of Galilee, why are you looking up like that to see Jesus? Go home. It is there that you will find him. You will not find him in the sky!"

We, too, can look for God where we can find him — around us here on earth.

The Meaning of Things

There is a story about a Chinese emperor called Ming. Once a wise man named Lao came to visit him. The emperor took his guest on a tour of the royal palace to show all he had—his spacious dwelling, his gardens, his wife, his children, his horses, his house-temple.

But the wise man seemed rather bored with it all and yawned several times while Ming was showing off his treasures. That evening the emperor gave a grand dinner for his guest. They sat opposite each other at the royal banquet, eating the finest and rarest of foods and drinking the choicest of wines. Servants ran to and fro, waiting upon them. While they were at the banquet, the wise man, Lao, suddenly asked his host whether he might like to make a journey with him. The emperor answered enthusiastically, "Oh, yes!"

"Hold on to the tip of my cloak," said Lao. That is what Ming did, and off they flew. The wise man flew with Ming over high mountains and deep seas to a magnificent palace. In comparison, Ming's palace was like a tiny hovel. In Lao's palace everything was of gold, ivory, and crystal. There was music everywhere, and incense, and rich food, and drink.

Ming remained with Lao for many years, and each day there were new surprises—concerts, theater-plays, dancers, and so on. Ming asked himself how he had ever been able to live in the squalor of his own empire. But one day Lao said, "Let us go back." And back they went.

It was as if they were falling through an endless tunnel for days and days, until they were sitting again opposite each other at the very same table from which they had started their journey. The food was still hot. The servants were still running about.

The emperor could not understand what had happened to him. So while the wise man was busy with a piece of chicken, the emperor called his oldest servant and asked him, "What happened to me?" The old man shrugged his shoulders, "Nothing, Sire. You have been staring in front of you for a moment or so."

It is by means of this story that the Chinese tell one another that everything in this world is transient and passing, like the grass in the field, which Jesus said is here today and tomorrow dries up; or like the lilies, more beautiful than Solomon in all his array, that tomorrow fade and wither. That is true of everything in this world, of all we might have and possess.

It is, however, not true of ourselves and of the good we do. We shall live and remain forever; and the good we do shall also live on. That is why we should take ourselves and others very seriously, much more seriously than all those things that pass and are gone. We must make use of material things to live and to serve. Those things should remain the "means" they are intended to be to help us grow and become fruitful in this life.

All in God's Hands

In the year A.D. 979 the famous Rabbi Jochanan died. He was a distinguished Jewish scholar and teacher of Scripture. If we remember both his name and the date of his death, it is because he must have been a very influential scholar, long remembered for his wise sayings.

One of those sayings was this: "God has three keys in his hands: the key to rain, the key to the womb, and the key to raise the dead." Sometimes we human beings think that we can do absolutely everything with our modern science and technology. We dig mines to get at minerals; we use fertilizers to grow plants; we build hospitals to heal the sick. We can do so many things that we often think we can forget about God completely. That is what very many seem to have done.

Yet what Rabbi Jochanan said more than 1000 years ago remains true. We have no key to rain; we have no key to life; we have no key out of death. We have no control over our beginning; we have no control over our end; and we have no control over the span allotted between that beginning and that end. The idea might frighten us. It should not. On the contrary. It means that we are *upheld*. We are borne up. We are sustained and carried in a divine hand.

All this does not mean we are not responsible for what we do. It does not mean we should not exert thought and effort to care for ourselves, for others, and for the world. But it does mean that our past, our present, and our future are and remain in God's hands.

Jesus expressed this in another way. When his disciples worried about how they should pray, he said, "Pray like this; just say, 'Father!'" Centuries before, a prophet of the Old Testament had already said of God, "Even if a mother should forget the child of her womb, I your God will never forget you! I have written your name in the palm of my hand." Yes, God has written your name in the palm of his hand!

Comic Relief

Robert Muller is an undersecretary at the United Nations. His office is in the huge United Nations Headquarters in New York. Although he must be very busy, he has managed to find time to write several books. One book is called *Most of All, They Taught Me Happiness.* That book has a chapter entitled "A Day Without Laughter Is a Lost Day."

The author declares that laughter and jokes often save people from emotions such as anger, disgust, and fear. He remarked that this is true even at the level of the United Nations' meetings. "How many times," he writes, "have I not seen meetings where tensions rose among the delegates and officials representing different views, interests, and positions."

In his book he describes the scene:

> They are deadly serious. They look at each other like devouring animals. With all the might of their intelligence, they exaggerate their cases. They fortify their

positions. They make biting and sarcastic remarks. They escalate their arguments. They show their teeth. They clench their fists. You can feel the physical tension mount in the conference room. The onlookers remain silent, watching the fight, watching that old human game. The fighters start to interrupt each other. Eyebrows are raised to their highest possible points. Hairs are standing up. Mouths dry up. You can cut the tension in the room with a knife. Cigarettes are lit, puffed at, and forgotten sleeves are pulled up. The discussion becomes spiteful. And then the chairman of the meeting manages to crack a joke. There is laughter. Everyone laughs. The tension is diffused, and things immediately return to normal.

It is in this way that jokes are an important element in diplomacy. It is in this way that humor is an important element in ourselves, and laughter an important factor in our health. Experts tell us that laughter means total relaxation. When we laugh, all the muscles and nerves in our face and body relax. As they relax, our body receives a new infusion of energy.

One famous stomach surgeon uses laughter as a cure for ulcers. His clinic is equipped with a projection room in which he shows hilarious films to his patients. I was told that in Russia even doctors use laughter as a help in the healing of heart diseases.

Have you ever read Psalm 126 where God is said to make us laugh and forget all our worries? "When the Lord brought us back, it was like a dream! How we laughed! How we sang for joy!"

Laugh today. Crack a joke! Break the tension around you! Break the tension within you! Lift up your heart!

Remembering Mercy

There is an African story about the stranger sent by God to visit earth. The stranger met a leper. When the leper heard that his visitor had come from somewhere in heaven, he asked, "Would you be able to heal me?"

"Oh certainly, no problem," said the stranger. And he healed the leper out of mercy. But he added, "In seven years I am coming back to check on what you have done with your new health!"

The stranger continued his journey, and he came upon a blind man who cried out to him, "Have mercy, heal me!" He, too, was healed, and to him also the stranger said, "In seven years I will return to see what you have done with your health."

He went further and met a crippled man who asked him in his turn to be healed. To him also the stranger said, "Be healed, but in seven years I am going to return to see what you have done with your new legs."

Seven years passed and the stranger returned. He went first to the former leper. But before he knocked at his door, he changed himself into a leper. When he knocked and the door was opened, the stranger asked the former leper for mercy. The man seeing him as a leper chased him away, shouting, "Get out! I might catch your disease!" At that moment his visitor showed himself in full health and said, "Let that disease be with you again." Instantly, the former leper became a leper again.

The stranger then went to the former blind man. He knocked on his door and acted as if he were blind. When the man he had healed of his blindness seven years before opened the door, he said to the stranger hastily, "Get out, beggar, get lost! I have no time for you." At that moment his blindness returned.

The stranger continued on to visit the former crippled man. As he knocked on the door, the stranger appeared to be a cripple. The door opened, and the former crippled man looked out with smile. "Come in, come in! How fortunate that you knocked on my door today! Come in. Sit down! To-day I am expecting a stranger who healed me seven years ago. I am sure that today he will heal you, too!"

That man, who had learned to show mercy to others, remained healed.

We all need mercy. We need it because we have been hard on others. Others need it because they have been cruel to us. Only mercy can help and save us. Francis of Assisi said, "Where there is mercy and discernment, there is neither luxury nor a hardened heart." Be merciful and mercy will be shown you.

Digesting Bad News

There was a man who was unhappy because he always had stomach trouble. He had this trouble because he always ate the wrong food. He knew that if he spiced everything he ate with hot pepper sauce, he would have trouble, yet he went on reaching for the sauce as soon as he sat down at table.

Consequently, he was constantly complaining about his stomach. He didn't even care for the peppery stuff, but since pouring it over his food was a habit of long standing, he continued with a habit that made him sick, very, very sick.

A strange man, you might say. A foolish man, you might judge. That is true. He was strange, he was foolish, he was self-destructive. I am sure that no one of you would act like that. We are all very particular about the food we eat, as particular as we can be. We eat what makes us feel happy, restful, and contented. That is normal. Why don't we do the same with our minds?

The first thing very many of us do in the morning is to buy a morning paper. I don't know which one you buy, but it doesn't matter because they are all pretty much the same — they all carry loads of bad news! Most probably the headlines will be about a disaster, a scandal, a crime, or something like that. That kind of news is not limited to the front page but is carried all through the newspaper.

Constant reading of depressing, bad, and cruel events can fill your mind and your imagination. You can become depressed yourself, negative, cynical, and sad if you are not careful. Your mind will be filled with toxic material even before you are well into beginning your day.

That is why we should be on the alert while reading the papers so that we do not allow our thoughts to be "polluted" by all that bad news. Read the bad news with suspicion. Humanity is not "merely bad." You yourself are not "merely bad news" either.

Isn't that what we affirm when we greet each other? "How are you?" "Fine, thank you." Paul wrote to the Ephesians: "Be filled with the Holy Spirit; speak to one another in the words of praise, thanking God for everything." So be careful about how you read your newspapers today. Read the positive, good news.

The Need to Be Needed

Did you ever hear the name Abbe Pierre? He became famous about thirty years ago. Abbe Pierre started a movement in France that soon spread throughout Europe and to other parts of the world. He began by encouraging groups of very poor people to organize to help themselves. The people began collecting garbage, paper, old bottles, scrap metal, and all kinds of other thrown-away things. Selling these materials, they were able to help themselves and to help other people who were poorer than themselves.

What I wanted to tell you about was how Father Pierre got his idea to start that work. He began it right after the Second World War. After four years of war and bombing, the town where he lived was in shambles. His parish was located in a slum area. Nothing worked. Water, sewage, electricity, transportation, everything was damaged. The people of the parish were miserably poor, without hope, living from day to day—no plans, no future, nothing. There was a general atmosphere of total despair. Abbe Pierre himself was ill, malnourished, and overworked. Life in the aftermath of war seemed bleak indeed.

Then one night the police phoned him. They asked him to visit a shabby lodging where they had found a man who had slashed his wrists to end his life. He went to the bed of the dying man and sat down beside him but could find no words of comfort or consolation.

Almost in tears, he said to the dying man, "My poor fellow, how can I expect to help you when I am in such desperate need of help myself!" The man in the bed opened his eyes, and there seemed to be a flicker of interest in them. He said with a broken voice, "Father, are you telling me that you need my help?"

"Yes, I think so," said Abbe Pierre. And he went on to confide to the dying man his own feelings of misery and dispair. The man on the bed listened, then he took the hand of Abbe Pierre and began to console and strengthen him. At the end of their long visit, the dying man said, "Father, you are the only one who ever needed me! The only one!"

It was at that moment that Abbe Pierre understood that so many people in this world need to be needed, that the world holds a multitude of people who crave to help others, who want to be full, useful human beings and to be part of the celebration life. That is why he started to organize the poor so that they could help others.

Come, Holy Spirit

Do you ever enter into yourself? It is quite an experience, and it can be done by everyone. Some time ago, I was in a class-room with school children between the ages of ten and twelve. Healthy little human beings are very lively at that age, as you know; and I saw how easily they managed.

I don't know whether you have any time just now, maybe you are preparing to get breakfast, or getting ready for work. But if you have a couple of minutes of free time, just sit down for a moment. Sit down comfortably. The most comfortable way to sit is straight up on a straight chair or on a stool.

Come to rest. Get relaxed. You can relax by raising your arm and letting it fall on your leg. Take care that before you drop your arm, you check to see whether you might hit a table or a chair! Don't put your arm down, simply let it fall. If you do it correctly, you will feel relaxed.

Now close your eyes and listen to all the sounds around you. All of them. The sounds of the house, the sounds of the street, the sounds of the birds outside. Maybe there are even other sounds. Let those penetrate you completely, become aware of all of them. Just sit there, and listen, listen, listen. . . .

You will find that you are becoming very, very quiet. After some time, it will be as if you are entering your own mind and your own spirit, deeper and deeper . . . .

One of the children said after her experience, "It was as if I fell into myself." You are entering your entire being, and now it becomes very easy to pray. Take just one word or phrase, like "Jesus," or "Our Father," or "Come, Holy Spirit." And in a completely relaxed state, say those words while breathing in, breathing out, slowly, deeply: "Come, Holy Spirit. Come, Holy Spirit."

After some time, a moment or two, you will feel refreshed. You have entered into yourself, into the deeper stream of your life, into harmony, serenity, bliss, peace, a great, great peace.

This type of centering prayer offers the surest way to happiness. Try it. Perhaps not at this moment; you may be in a hurry. But try it when you are free and at ease. In that way you will be able to pray always, everywhere, in whatever situation—in the bus, at home, in church, anywhere. As Saint Paul advised the Thessalonians to do: "Be joyful always; pray at all times!" There is no greater way to lift up your heart!

Handling Conflicts

How do you solve a conflict? Many of you may have a conflict at the moment with someone or other—maybe with your spouse, with your child, or with a friend, with your boss, or with a colleague. What do you do in such a case? Many of us go about it the wrong way.

Take the case of a husband and his wife. He really has some serious complaints about her. But because he doesn't know how to handle the situation, he keeps his mouth shut. He buries the issue deep inside.

The wife has some serious difficulties with him. But because she doesn't know how to handle the situation either, she, too, keeps her mouth shut. She buries everything inside. New problems arise, new difficulties crop up. Neither of the two speaks. They both suffer and bear it in silence. Their relationship does not improve.

The husband comes home later and later. She is more and more absent. They scarcely embrace each other any more. They rarely speak to each other. Then one day there is an issue between the two that becomes the drop that makes the bucket overflow. He starts to shout, she starts to shout. "You remember ten years ago you did this, five years ago you did that, eight years ago . . . ."

The shouting match is horrendous. The neighbors are astonished. It lasts and lasts. Everything comes out. And in the end, so many things have been said that the two do not know what to do next. In the bedroom their children, wakened by the noise of the quarrel, are sobbing in fright.

How can we prevent situations like this? We can do that by listening to a very simple piece of advice given by Jesus himself. He said, "Let not the sun go down upon your anger." Solve your problems before the day is over. That is what we can do. We should speak about our problems as soon as they arise.

But, even then, be careful to chose the right moment. Statistics show that most family quarrels begin just before or during meals. For very obvious reasons, everyone feels hungry, and tired, and a little depressed. The sugar level in our blood is minimal, offering optimum conditions for an ugly scene.

So when there is an issue, wait until after the meal. Sit down then and try to explain your difficulties to each other. Try to solve them. The neighbors will not be disturbed. Your children will sleep with that sense of security which they need in order to grow. And all will be well before the day is over.

Worthless Worries

Many people worry. Most probably, all people worry. They worry about all kinds of things. They feel a slight pain in their chest and think, "Something is wrong with my heart." They get a pimple to the right of their nose and say, "Skin cancer!" They said something in the dark and are afraid it was overheard. They have to make a trip, and they imagine all the things that could happen: blow-outs, overturned cars, head-on collisions, and so on.

Many of the worries people have are about the future. When we start to worry about the future, an endless field of possibilities opens before us because we imagine all the kinds of things that can happen. If we gave in to all those worries, we would not survive. We would freeze on the spot. We would not be able to move. We would never be able to take any risk in life.

We should, therefore, get rid of those worries. We have all had worries that proved to be silly in the end. The pain in our chest disappeared by itself. The pimple to the right side of our nose vanished without leaving a trace. Nobody overheard what we said in the dark. The car we were traveling in had no blow-outs, no head-on collisions.

Is it not true to say that ninety percent of our worries were a loss of time and energy? There are, of course, justified worries. But there are so many worries that are only figments of our imagination. Jesus said something about all this. "Do not worry about tomorrow. The worries of today are enough." He, of course, added something else. "Do not worry. All the hairs on your head are counted!"

Sharing Religious Experiences

Did you ever have a religious experience? Researchers recently have been posing that question to people all around the globe, and they came up with some astonishing statistics.

In Great Britain, a country not so well known for its religiosity, forty-four percent of the people interviewed said they were convinced that they had had a religious experience. Another thirty percent thought they had had a religious experience. That means that over seventy-four percent of the population in Britain was conscious of having had religious experiences during their lives.

Did you ever have one? It would be interesting to know. It would be interesting for yourself, too. It would mean that you have had access to divinity, to the sacred, to the holy.

About seven hundred years ago, a man who specialized in religious experiences, Saint Bernard of Clairvaux, made the remark that it would be beneficial if everyone "would drink spiritually from his own well." We should not always rely on the spirituality of others, on the spiritual insights of a King David, of a Jeremiah, of a Paul, or other people of the past.

Some time ago, a group of people came together to exchange ideas about the mystery of God. They, too, asked one another whether they had ever had a religious experience. They learned that they had.

A Sister told the group that as a small girl she had been walking one day through an open field when she came to a brook. The water was not very deep so she took off her shoes and socks and stepped barefoot into the clear water. She saw the sun shining through the water on her bare feet, and she suddenly felt that all was well with the world, that God holds all things together in his care.

Another told how one evening he was riding home in a bus. While descending the last slope into town, the driver lost control of the brakes. The passengers in the bus noticed it immediately and started to scream. "And then," our friend told us, "I suddenly felt very calm. I said to myself, I am in the hands of God. And I felt it was true. All the others screamed again when the bus, braking on the motor in its first gear, came to a stop in a shallow ditch alongside the road. Everyone escaped unharmed."

I am sure that many of us have had such experiences. We should cherish them and tell them to our children and our parents. The remembrance of them may help us and others through the difficulties of life and will keep our hearts uplifted, high above the worries of everyday life.

An Encouraging Word

A father and his son were walking through a field during a hiking trip very far from home in a place they had never been before. The place seemed to be totally deserted. They had met no one during their climb. At a certain point they came to a kind of ditch that extended as far as they could see. At first they hesitated, wondering whether they should turn back, or attempt to leap across it. Finally they decided to attempt the jump.

The father jumped first. He landed with his feet in a hole he had not seen, hidden as it was by the tall grass. His foot became embedded. He tried to pull it out. But the more he struggled to extricate himself, the tighter the foot was wedged in. The father who now desperately needed his son's help shouted, "Son you must get over here and help me or I will never get out!" And then he added, "But you will never make it over! You don't have the strength! You don't have the nerve. You are no use to me. You will never do it. You are a weakling, a clod, a coward, a failure."

Do you think, in all honesty, that that man's son would then be able to jump across that ditch? Not unless he possessed extraordinary belief in himself!

How many people have the strength to succeed entirely on their own without encouragement from others, against the odds of others' cynical disbeliefs? We need encouragement from others. And so do those who live with us.

There is little point in paying school tuitions for your children, then telling them every day that they are stupid, lazy, useless. Or telling them by word or manner, "I am sure you are never going to make it!"

There is no use while bringing someone to the hospital, saying all along the way, "I'm afraid you aren't going to make it; I think you are going to die!" It is no good giving someone a task to do, then saying to him, "I doubt you can carry it through; you'll probably fail!"

We should encourage rather than dishearten, blame or humiliate one another. That must have been the reason Saint Paul wrote so often in his letters: "Encourage one another! Strengthen one another! Support one another!"

Think of that today and speak an encouraging word to your son, to your daughter, to your wife, to your husband, to the ones you meet. It will do them good, and you, too!

God's Gifts

I had just finished giving a talk to about five hundred students at a secondary school in Kikuyu, a village near Nairobi, the capital of Kenya. For several years I had been giving these talks at the invitation of the Theological Association of Alliance High School.

This talk was to be the last one. In a few days I was going to leave the country. After the talk, the students and teachers gathered around for the usual cup of tea and informal discussion and answering of questions—some of them difficult. But now the last question had been asked and answered, and it was time to leave.

As I walked to my car, it was dark outside. I turned on the ignition, switched on the lights, and prepared to back out cautiously onto the road when I heard a knock at the car window. A student, a girl of about fifteen, was standing there. I rolled down the window, and she said, "We are so grateful. You have been such a gift from God to us!"

I have forgotten most of the details of that evening, but the tone of that voice and the words that she said I will never forget. Without realizing it, that young girl had expressed in those last minutes in the dark of that tropical night, a central insight of African spirituality—we are intended by God to be gifts to one another!

A South African theologian, Manasse Buthelezi, has written a book developing this thought, carefully worked out and rather technical and lengthy. As with so many theological works, it lacks the directness of daily life. That young high school girl, whose name I will never know, summed it up so beautifully. We are God's gifts to one another. The gift which each one is, is unique, irreplaceable! That is why we are all so gloriously, fantastically different. You, yes, you are God's gift to those around you!

All in Everything

Did you ever fall in love? I hope you did. It is such a revealing experience. Even if you never have, you may have noticed what happened to others when they did.

Someone in love sees the whole world in the light of the loved one. "Every time I see a flower, I am seeing you! Every time I hear a song, I am hearing you! Every time I touch a lovely thing, I am touching you! Every time I feel the cool, refreshing rain after a hot and dusty day, I feel the loveliness of you. I find you in everything, and through everything, and with everything!" There is yet another refrain: "I am willing to give my life for you. I am willing to die for you!"

How often have people written that to one another. How often have those words passed through telephone wires and via satellites echoed around the world, again, and again, and again.

Do you realize that these words describe how God loves. How he loves all of us. How he loves you—*you!* In that way, and in no other way. The word "love" can be deceptive. But the love of a real friend is not deceptive. A real friend knows what it means to love. It means to will, to hope for, to desire the growth, the happiness, the fulfillment, of the beloved one. In essence, love is power, dynamism, energy.

God showed us all this in Jesus, our dearest and truest friend, our brother, the one for whose love we have all been created.

You say that you feel lonely, somber, frustrated, at a loss, useless. Are you not deceiving yourself, really? Are you not forgetting that the substance of your life is this love God has for you? God sees you in all and everything. He created it all for you. It seems unbelievable. "I can't believe that you love me in the way you do!" Isn't that what all loved ones say?

Brother Death

Some people say that it is not wise to speak about death. They think that to speak about death provokes death. There was a researcher at the university who wanted to study the funeral customs somewhere in Zambia, Africa. The people there told him not to do it. It was too dangerous. If you think that that is true, you had better not read on. Sorry for having brought up the subject.

But not everyone thinks about death as some kind of disaster. Francis of Assisi said of death: "Be praised, my Lord, for our brother Death, from whom no man among the living can escape!" Francis was convinced that death is birth into a new life for those who live in God's love. He compared death to the birth of a baby from the womb. When a baby is forced out of the womb of its mother, it must also think that it is dying. Everything has changed. Supports are gone. All protection seems to have fallen away. No wonder that every baby starts to cry after birth into this world.

Out of this world we will be born again into a new world. Francis said often that death should remind us of the role which we are expected to play here in this world. Death should make us reflect upon our lives here and now. In a letter which he addressed to all magistrates, councilors, judges, and governors around the world, and to all persons whom this letter would reach, he wrote:

> Take note, and reflect that the day of death is approaching. So I ask you with whatever reverence I can that the cares and the worries of this world which you have may not cause you to forget God or turn from the path of his commandments, for all those who forget him and turn away from his commandments are cursed and shall be assigned by him to oblivion. And when their day of death arrives, everything they thought they had shall be taken away from them.

But if we live well, we shall be born into joy, all together, and that reunion of the family of God will never end but last forever.

The Simple Approach

There is a famous Flemish theologian with a name almost as difficult as his theology, Edward Schillebeeckx. Some years ago he wrote two books about Jesus, one of 640 pages in length, and a second of over 900 pages. To prepare himself for writing these long volumes about the life and words of Jesus, he studied for two solid years all kinds of exegetical works, adding the result of those readings to all the endless studies that had gone before.

All that theological work is admirable. It is also necessary. Theologians have their role to play. But sometimes it is not much of a help in our immediate daily life. Each day, year in and year out, we need to approach Jesus directly, to listen to him, to watch him, to observe how he approached daily living.

Look at the birds, look at the flowers, at the sun, at the rain, at playing children, Jesus would say. Listen to that boy playing his flute, to the girls singing their songs and dancing their rounds. Taste the goodness of water, of bread, and of wine, especially the wine I gave them at Cana!

Jesus' approach to daily living seems so much simpler, the simplest. He lived in that very simple, enjoyable way, loving, simply loving life. That must have been one of the main reasons why people around him started to understand that he came from God, for God is the greatest lover of life. People began to understand that Jesus was like God, was God. He loved them. He loved life; he loved all of it. He even said that he did not want to lose any of it.

Isn't that divine? It is, and we should participate in that simplest of joys—enjoying life, its greatness and its intimacy to the full. "Let the sea thunder and all that it holds and the world with all who live in it; let the rivers clap their hands and the mountains shout for joy" (Psalm 98:7-8).

What's Your Opinion?

Jesus was surrounded that day by his followers. In general they were simple people, most of them fishermen, with the smell of fish in their hair and their clothing. They were the people that did not seem to play any part in human history, the non-participants. Nobodies in the eyes of the leaders, ecclesial and political. Nobody ever asked for their opinion. Their opinion did not count. Their lives did not count. They were like so many of us—objects of decrees, laws, and decisions made by others.

That day Jesus turned to them. He addressed them. He asked them for their opinion. They were surprised. Nobody of any importance had ever done that before. And Jesus was very important; otherwise, they would not have followed him. He asked for their opinion. They could not believe their ears. He asked them, "Who do you think I am?"

Of course, he could not really be interested in *their opinion*, so they answered, "Some say you are John the Baptist;

others say you are Jeremiah, or Elijah, or a prophet . . . ."
He interrupted them. He said, "All right. That is what the
others say. What do you say?"

There must have been a moment of silence. This was
totally new. This was unheard of. Finally, Peter understood.
"You are our Savior. You are the Son of God." Jesus looked
at him and said, "Simon, you spoke very well. Don't think,
however, that this idea came from you. It comes from my
Father working in you." Peter, that apparently simple fisher-
man, smelling of whitefish and sea water, filled with God!

When I would ask you, "Who do you think Jesus is?"
many of you would answer, I am sure, like Simon Peter, "He
is the Messiah, our Savior." And Jesus would say of you,
too, "Don't make the mistake that that idea comes from you.
It comes from my Father working in you!"

The Father, God, God's Spirit working in you! Good
gracious!

The Power in Forgiveness

It was in Maasai country on one of those vast African plains. A son had offended his father. He had refused to show the respect due to him, to the one who had given him life, and who, according to the traditional African idea, was still giving him life.

The father had broken with his son, as the son had broken with the father. The son, considered to be a threat to the whole community, was obliged to leave the village, banished by the people. He remained outside the village.

Every night the father would climb a hill to pray in the loneliness of the African night. He prayed for the power to be able to forgive his son, the power to restore his lifebond with him. Again and again, he came down in the morning without his prayer being answered. Outside the manyatta (village compound), the son was waiting. Avoided by all, he was withering away.

One morning the father came down a changed man. His prayer had been heard; he had received the power to forgive. The good news spread like wildfire. The elders came together. The son was informed by his age mates. The whole village gathered. Father and son met in the midst of the community. They all looked on while that father restored the lifebond with his son. Everyone began to sing and to dance. Life had been restored.

Forgiveness is so important. It is the only way we can make up for the past. That is why Jesus said on his first appearance to his disciples after his resurrection, "Peace be with you! Peace. I give you the power to forgive!"

The power to forgive, this is what that Maasai father had to pray for.

Looking for You

James was an adopted child, an orphan. Everyone in his adoptive family had tried to make his life as happy as possible, but in some way James felt that he was an outsider in the family of six.

One evening James did not return home. At first, hardly anyone noticed. But when it grew later and later, the family became worried. Where could he be? What could have happened to him? Had he been kidnaped? Had he had some kind of accident? Had he run away?

After some hesitation, they decided to call the police. A search began all over the neighborhood. No James. When morning came, he still had not been found. The search went on. His friends at school were questioned to discover whether they might have some clue as to where he might be.

Finally a boy was found who said, "I think I know a place where he used to go sometimes." He led the parents out of town and along an unused road that ran beside a railroad track. After an hour's long walk, the boy pointed to an old wrecked car left in the undergrowth of a bush, and said, "He might be in there."

The parents, tired as they were, started to run toward the old car. When they looked inside, they found him, sound asleep. His mother, in tears, roused him. At first James looked frightened, but when he saw who it was, he broke into a happy smile.

"James," his mother cried, "Whatever happened to you? Why did you do this to us? Why?"

James climbed out of the car and flung his arms about her, smiling and sobbing at the same time. He buried his face in her shoulder, but his father, tired and relieved, heard him say, "I wanted to know whether you would come to look for me. I wanted to see whether you really loved me."

Sometimes it seems that God suddenly disappears from our lives. We can't seem to find God at all. Is God testing us at those times? Perhaps. Did Jesus not do the same at times? Sometimes he went apart from his friends, and his disciples had to go looking for him. And that is what they did. We should do the same.

Praying (1)

When did you pray last? I don't mean just sitting in a church. I mean when did you really *pray?* Was it a long time ago? Why was it so long ago? "Because it is so difficult," you say? Too many people have decided that prayer is "too difficult" for them. You can see the result of that in the bookstores— shelves filled with books on "how to pray."

I sometimes think it is a plot, propaganda to spread the idea that prayer is difficult. People begin to believe it, and now they say so readily, "I'm not good at prayer, you know."

Is prayer really so difficult? I wonder. I wonder because we pray so frequently during the day. Not to God, that is true, but to one another. When I am in my office at the University, all kinds of people come in for all kinds of reasons. John wants a letter of recommendation. Stephen asks for some money to visit his sick mother. Catherine comes to borrow a stapling machine. Anne wants something else. It goes on and on. It simply does not stop.

They don't come in to command me; they can't order me. They don't come to tell me a story, though sometimes they do that, too. They come to ask me a favor. And that is a kind of prayer; in a way, they are praying. They look at me to catch my attention. They contemplate me. They ask a favor, they petition. They tell me how kind I am supposed to be. They say, "Everybody told me I should come to you." In a way they even adore me. They say, "If you can't help me, what am I supposed to do? Who is going to help me?" They ask pardon for the inconveniences they are causing me. They offer me something: a handshake, a smile, a flower. They promise that it will only be for this one time, that they will not ask again, which, of course, is not true. They pray, and they make me hear their prayers. They are astonishingly good at that.

If I needed something from you, I would come to you, too, using all the techniques and skills I have just described. We all know these techniques. We know them very well!

So it is not true to say that we cannot pray "because it is so difficult." It is easy. It comes naturally. There must be another reason why praying to God is so difficult. There is another reason.

Praying (2)

Praying is risky. Praying is dangerous. If we pray, we draw near to God. God always takes advantage of these often-too-rare occasions. Once we put ourselves within his reach, God is going to touch us. Oh yes, God does. To touch God and to be touched by God is no light matter.

I will give you an example, although you, yourself, are the best example. Have you never noticed that every time you sit, or stand, or kneel to pray you always get a message or a task, an insight or an inspiration? That is why praying is so risky. That is why it is so difficult.

Take Moses. He saw the burning bush. Something very mysterious. Something very holy. He grew curious. He put off his sandals, and barefoot, on tiptoe, he drew closer to this appearance of God. He should never have done that. He should have known better. He should have run away as fast as he could if he wanted to continue his ordinary life.

He did not. He listened. He contacted God, he prayed. He touched God, and immediately God touched him. God really does not lose a chance. God gave him a task, a very hard one. God said, "Moses, lead my people out of Egypt."

Moses, frightened, answered in protest, "How can you expect me to do a thing like that?" But it was too late. Moses had prayed and he had been caught. He tried to save the situation; he protested, "Listen to my speech, and you will hear that I am no orator!" God said, "Take your brother Aaron with you; let him do the talking."

If you pray, you will be caught, too. If you grant yourself the time to approach God, you are going to know what you are supposed to do. If you do not want to know that, then don't pray.

Yet, how would we be able to live without prayer? How could we live without ever being touched by the divine hands that brought us into being? Would you not like to be drawn closer to your divine life source? Is that not what we are all hoping for in the depths of our hearts? Is it not God himself who is waiting there for us?

Your Own Prayer

One day a young Jewish student named Michael was seated in the synagogue, engrossed in a study of the Holy Scriptures. Around him, in that place of prayer, others of the faithful came and went. Michael was absorbed in his study, but occasionally caught an echo of a prayer here and there, spoken aloud, as often happens in a synagogue.

One prayer, spoken by a stranger, suddenly caught his attention. The stranger prayed, "Oh God, please remain with me when I know that I need you; but please don't leave me when I don't feel that need!" Michael was deeply touched by that prayer. So much so that he related his experience to his teacher, Kalman.

His teacher's face lighted with enthusiasm and he cried out, full of joy, "Michael I want you to repeat what you have told me." Michael repeated it. Kalman reiterated, "Tell it to me once more ... Once more ..." He made Michael repeat his story seven times. Later on that day, Michael found a moment to ask his professor for an explanation of his strange insistence.

The old man placed a kindly hand on Michael's arm and he said, "Every human being has a spirit that is uniquely his own. It is sometimes difficult to recognize that spirit and that prayer. When you were so deeply touched by the prayer of that stranger, I knew that you had found your prayer. Michael, you have found it!"

We, too, should find our prayer. We never find anything if we do not look for it. That is why we should be very attentive to what we experience, to what moves us deeply.

One day you will find your prayer. And finding it, you will find your spirit, yourself!

Distractions Are Prayer

There is a venerable old story about some students some-where in an old Polish town who asked their teacher about wisdom. They had reason to ask; they had heard that a man reputed to be very wise had come to live not far from them. The students wanted to know how they could find out whether the newcomer was really as wise as people said he was.

Their teacher, Israel Ben Elieser, gave them this answer: "To find out whether he is really wise, ask him the following question, 'How can we overcome distractions and worldly thoughts during prayer and meditation on Holy Scripture?' If he gives you advice on how to overcome them, forget about him. He is neither wise nor holy." The students were much surprised. That was one of the questions they had planned to ask the wise man, for they felt themselves so often hindered in their prayers by distraction and worldly thoughts. They asked their teacher for an explanation.

Rabbi Israel Ben Elieser responded, "What we human beings should do constantly is to lift anything that is of this world high up toward God."

So many people of good will complain about distractions during prayer. Many even give up prayer because of them. They do not realize that those distractions come from God. They come from the Holy Spirit. They bring us back to every-day reality when we are trying to find holiness outside of daily life. We are, we think, lifting our hearts up to God and then find ourselves interrupted by thoughts about our work, our relationships, our loves, and our antipathies.

Yet it is in that world that we live; it is in that world that we should find our holiness and our fulfillment. It is the world of our everyday life that should become penetrated with God's love. Distractions are more often than not God's invitations to us; they are God's grace.

The Ground of Our Being

It was a grim scene. Even the curious and the sensation-seekers must have felt it. It was somewhere in the middle of Africa, though it could just as well have been in so many parts of the world. A dozen men had been summarily condemned to death. Today was the day set for the public execution. The government wanted to set an example.

At the end of the field where the curious crowd had gathered, the military had set up twelve oil drums filled with sand. The men to be executed were to be bound to those drums.

Everything was ready. Everyone was waiting. The noise of the crowd had subsided; the sense of the tragedy was growing.

In the distance, growing louder, one could hear the muffled roar of the approaching army trucks; yet, mingled with that sound there was, strangely enough, the sound of singing. The trucks came nearer. They were now in full view. The twelve condemned prisoners, seated among their armed guards, were singing. At first one could not distinguish the words of their song. But soon the words became recognizable.

"You have accused us, but we are innocent. You do not believe us. You do not respect us. God does. God will defend us, the giver of our lives, the guardian of our rights."

The prisoners repeated the refrain over and over again. The crowd had grown completely silent. The only words audible were some harsh, clipped military commands. The bystanders had begun to feel uncomfortable. Some left the scene.

When the prisoners had been bound to the drums, they began to sing again, this time an old hymn known all over English speaking Africa, "What a friend we have in Jesus!" They knew that they were safe in God's hands, though delivered into the hands of men. They were safe with God, the lasting ground of our being.

Like a Lily of the Field

Sister Elizabeth was a nun of a solemn, conventional, cloistered Order. But Sister Elizabeth was not solemn! She loved plants, trees, animals, flowers, and even fish. She loved all living things so much she brought some of them into her room so that she could have them very near her. Her room was filled with plants. She had a tiny aquarium; no one knew where it came from, but there it was. She also had a canary in a cage that once in a while sang at the wrong time. The canary felt so much at home, it made little difference whether the door of the cage were opened or closed.

Some of the other Sisters worried about Sister Elizabeth. The Abbess, too. Wasn't Sister Elizabeth becoming too distracted by all this, too dissipated? Wasn't she in danger of losing her vocation of being for the Lord, and only for the Lord? Occasionally they discussed the problem of Sister Elizabeth in her absence. That is why, one day, the Abbess decided to talk to her personally. Abbesses are sometimes very good at that.

When she entered Sister Elizabeth's room, the fish in the aquarium were just having their lunch. The Abbess sat down and was silent for a time. (How do you tackle a problem like this one?) She began to feel a bit ridiculous. Elizabeth sat down, too.

Finally the Abbess said, "Why do you have all these things in your room? Don't they take too much of your time? Don't they distract you too much in your prayers?"

Sister Elizabeth looked up at her and answered, "Distract me? Not at all. On the contrary, they help me to pray and to work."

She went to a corner of her monastic cell, took a book, the Book, and said, "Should we study the examples Jesus gave us?" She opened her Bible and read, "Consider the flowers in the field . . . ." "Look at the birds . . . ." She stopped, and asked, "How can I be like a flower in the field, having no care but to praise the Lord; how can I be like the tiny bird, the little sparrow, whom the Lord does not forget if I have nothing near at hand to remind me?"

She pointed at her plants, the fish, and the birds. "See how they enjoy the life they have from God. They speak constantly of him!"

The Abbess, disconcerted, said only, "Well, I hope . . . ."

"Yes," said Sister Elizabeth, "Hope! That is what they are teaching me, too!"

Opening the Circle

So many of us feel trapped in one way or another, trapped, chained, fenced in, and caught in a small circle without too much hope. We would like to liberate ourselves, to live another type of life, broader, wider, larger, deeper, higher, fuller. Deep down within ourselves we know that we would be able to do it, but we don't. Only some of us seem able to break through the constricting circle in which we live.

One of those who broke through is very well known. We've mentioned him several times. His real name was John, but nobody called him John. They all called him by his nickname, Francesco, Francese, the Frenchman. And that is how that name came in the list of saints.

He was born in Assisi in Italy. As we all know he was a rich young man, the son of the wealthiest textile baron in town. In that time, people had not very many things to spend their money on. They spent it all on clothing. Francis was rather small of stature, but very intelligent, and a heartbreaker —plenty of parties, plenty of money, plenty of drinks, plenty of girls. He was not too successful as a soldier, but he made up for it by his romantic adventures, his smashing clothes, his beautiful feathered hats, and his fashionable high-heeled boots.

And yet he was unhappy. He felt himself hemmed in. He, too, was caught in a small constricting circle. He was at a loss until he decided to start a new life, a wider life, a broader life, a life fulfilled. He made the final step into that new life by a kiss.

One day he encountered a man of a kind he had feared and avoided up to that moment, the kind of person who had been excluded from the circle in which he had lived. He met . . . a leper.

Francis stepped from his horse, went to that man, and took his hand. He kissed him first on his face and then on his mouth. The small circle in which he had been living split wide open.

Maybe, maybe he could be a model to us. Not that we have to kiss a leper, but we have to break open that small circle in which we live.

Called to His Supper

They formed a community, a very mixed community. Fathers, mothers, children, a priest, some religious, a student. In a way, they were always together; and in a way, they were hardly ever together because they had different jobs and very diverse working hours.

Once a week, they were definitely all together, Saturday evening. They had made it a point that, whatever happened, Saturday evening should be kept free for an evening meal together. The cooking for that evening was done with the greatest care. The birthdays of the week were celebrated that evening, and any other important events—success in an exam, a new tooth, a prayer heard, recovery from an illness, a task completed.

Everyone looked forward to that meal. It was the crowning event of the week, the harbinger of Sunday peace, leisure, and companionship. It was a source of encouragement for each one, all through the week. It made the tasks and difficulties of the week less burdensome.

It is to such a meal, at the close of our days, our work week here on earth that Jesus invites us. We are reminded of that Final Supper during the celebration of the Eucharist, when just before communion the priest prays, "Happy are those who are called to his Supper!"

When some priests are celebrating in the morning, they sometimes change the text to "Happy are those who are called to this meal." That is a pity and a mistake. It loses sight of the great promise of the Lord. It overlooks our expectation and our hope of reunion with Jesus and our loved ones.

We are happy, and we should be happy *now* because we have something to look forward to. One day we will celebrate the Supper of the Lord together in our everlasting home. How happy we are!

He Calls Us Friends

We are accustomed to call each other brothers and sisters. It is a custom as old as Christianity. We do it because Jesus told us that God is our Father. We are often led to think that this brother/sister relationship is the best expression of love. What could be more intimate, closer than being brothers and sisters to one another. Yet we all know that sisters and brothers do not always enjoy the best of relationships.

That is true in everyday life. It is also true in the Scriptures. The first couple of brothers mentioned in the Old Testament were so jealous that Cain killed Abel. Jacob swindled Esau out of his heritage. Joseph was sold by his brothers.

We find the same in the stories of the New Testament. It is true even of Jesus. His brothers came one day to the place where he was teaching to take him back home. They said, and the Gospels tell us, that because Jesus was exaggerating things, they thought he had gone mad! Almost every time

Jesus speaks about brothers in his recommendations and parables, those brothers are causing trouble! We have to forgive them seventy times seven times. We have to overlook the splinter in their eye.

As far as I know, Jesus never called us his brothers and sisters, except in the one case where he called us also his mother! Jesus calls us by another name. He characterizes us in a different way. He thinks of us differently. Jesus calls us *friends*. He calls us by the word that indicates the deepest love relationship that can exist between human beings.

Husbands and wives are not always friends; brothers and sisters are not necessarily friends; even lovers are sometimes not friends.

Real friendship is rare. We are friends in so far as we are in the other, and the other is in us. Jesus calls us friends. That is why he did not hesitate to give his life for us—for you, for me.

God befriending me! How proud we should be, and how humble at the same time.

A Balm for All Wounds

Etty Hillesum was twenty-nine years old when she disappeared from the human scene. We have a letter from the person who saw her disappear aboard a train bound for Auschwitz, the Nazi extermination camp for Jews in Poland. Etty knew where she was going. Etty was well versed in literature and taught Russian. She loved the letters of Rainer Maria Rilke and the New Testament. She enjoyed the earthiness of human life. She was a liberated woman. There is no doubt about that when you read her diaries, published under the title *An Interrupted Life* (Washington Square Press, Pocket Books: New York, 1985). She was a loving, sensitive person. She must have been a marvelous friend.

During her studies of the great Russian authors and under the influence of events happening around her, Etty rapidly developed into a person who was able to see the good in all the circumstances and persons she met in her life. Even in those who would lead her to her earthly undoing, even in the cruellest and most frustrated ones, she could still discern a trace of the handiwork of their Creator, a fingerprint of God. She called it "just a little piece of God."

She wrote:

> And that is when my task begins. It is not enough simply to proclaim you, my God, to commend you to the hearts of others. I must also try to clear the path for them in their journey toward you . . . .
>
> Every soul must become a dwelling dedicated to you, O God. And I promise you, yes, I promise that I will try to find a dwelling place and a refuge for you in as many hearts as possible.

Until the end, that is what she tried to do. It is a beautiful description of the task that all of us have in life. Are we not called to find God in ourselves, in others, in the whole world? Is it not the one thing we all share in common—the "being in God"—the marvelous reality that will unite us all together?

Etty finished her diary on the twelfth of September 1943. She died on November thirtieth of that year. She was gassed and cremated. One year before she died she had written, "We should be willing to act as balm for all wounds." Etty Hillesum is still playing that role of comforter for all who draw hope through her words and from her life.

He Liberates Us

She considered herself very plain, much plainer that her beautiful sisters. When she looked at herself in the mirror, she was not impressed. She was not jealous. She was too kind to be jealous. Even the loving kindness that was her special gift she did not recognize. How could she? Nobody had ever told her. People were nice to her, in the family, at school. It seemed, however, that everyone usually took her for granted, just as she did herself.

Then he met her. He shook hands with her very shyly. In the beginning they had very little to say to each other. She could not believe that anyone might really be interested in her. But he persisted in coming around, and gradually they spent more and more time together. In the end he even kissed her, but that is saying too much. He just brushed her cheek with his lips. Finally, he said, "Mary, I love you. I think of you all day. You are so good, you are so wise, you are so sweet. Oh, Mary, gosh!"

At first, she thought that he was joking. He wasn't. Finally she began to understand, not only with her brains, but with her heart. It changed her whole world. All kinds of thoughts she had never had before welled up within her. All kinds of possibilities, hidden in the foggy grey of what might be, came into the open. Looking at herself in the mirror again, she saw what he had made her see. She was beautiful, she was lovable, she was desirable, she was important.

The people who followed Jesus had no great idea of themselves, either. Think of a man like Zaccheus who, in his heart, considered himself a miser. Indeed he was a miser until he met Jesus, who looked straight in his eyes, and Zaccheus could see the love there. Jesus said to him, "Zaccheus, you are a real son of Abraham. Today I am going to visit you in your home."

Think of Mary Magdalen who considered herself to be a sinner. But Jesus said of her, "Nobody ever had a greater love!"

The light of understanding, the love in Jesus' eyes changed their lives completely. Whenever the light of Jesus fell upon a person around him, things became clear, options became obvious, and persons found themselves.

What will happen to you if you put yourself in that light, the light of Jesus that reveals to you your unique worth, that liberates you, that renders you in God's eyes most lovable!

Please Look

John and Mary had a misunderstanding. John did not like it. He was worried about it because he liked, no, he loved Mary very much. He had tried to talk to her, but the words would not come. He had telephoned her, but the moment he heard her voice, he grew panicky, forgot what he was going to say and put the phone down. He had written her a letter, but when he reread it, it wouldn't do, and he tore it up. Then he remembered that Mary liked flowers—roses, dark red roses. He went to a florist shop and bought one. One only because roses were very expensive, and he was far from rich. The florist added some green, and John wrapped the rose carefully in some nice thin paper. Carrying his rose, he arrived at her apartment a few minutes before Mary was due to arrive. He lay the rose on the doorsill. Then he waited, hidden around a corner.

Then she came. His heart jumped into his throat; his mouth grew suddenly dry, very dry. Mary went to her door, opened her purse, took out her key, unlocked the door and closed it behind her. She had not seen the rose.

John felt terribly disappointed. That is how God must feel so often about us. He has filled our lives with all kinds of goodness. He has filled the whole world with glory, and we don't notice a thing. We don't notice God's love at all.

Jesus said, "I played for you the flute, and you did not dance. You did not even hear me!"

Let us listen, and look. Let us see.

The Dragon Will Be Killed

Do you remember, when you were a child, how you loved to hear a story before you fell asleep? Even today children love to hear a story, despite radio and television. If you give them a chance, they will ask you, "Please, Dad, please, Mom, please, Grannie, tell me a story."

There is your child in bed with the favorite doll or teddy bear beside the curly head on the pillow, waiting for your story. You tell your tale. An old, old one with a terrible dragon or a horrible stepmother, or a voracious wolf, or with children left behind, lost in the forest.

Your child is listening, knowing that there will be a turn in the story at a certain point. The dragon will be killed. The stepmother will change. The wolf will be shot. The children will find their way home, helped by the birds. If you change your story, and the dragon is not killed, or the prince does not meet the princess, you will be told, "It's wrong, you told it wrong; it's not like that!"

Children like to hear before the day, with all its troubles, is over that in the end all will be well. Isn't that the story of Jesus on the cross, and his final resurrection? Of course it is. In the end all will be well. And for you, too.

Don't Mention God

He was the father of beautiful children. But now he was ill, close to death in a hospital. He had told me that he would like me to see him, but he had added, "Don't go talking to me about God, or the church, or religion." He had become embittered about all those things for reasons that were complex and do not matter now.

The day came when the doctor told his family that he had only a few more days to live. I visited him that day. I asked him, "How are you?" He said, "You know how I am. A few days and I will be finished."

I asked him, "And then ....?" He looked at me and said, "Nothing. That will be the end. There will be nothing."

A silence fell. I didn't know what to say. In that silence, we both looked into that mysterious bourn from which no one returns and that awaits us all.

Finally I found words. I stammered, "I don't know ... I have never been there either, but aren't there some signs and promises that give us hope? Our death is no greater a mystery than our birth. Are we not coming from, and returning to, the same Source of Life?"

He looked away, but he did not say, "Shut up," as he would have done some days before. I felt a bit encouraged and went on. "You yourself are the father of children. Wouldn't you always be willing to receive them in your home? Don't you think that there might be a Father who understands all?"

"Please, go away," he said. I left his room and went down the corridor to visit another patient. Then a nurse came over to me. "That patient you were visiting wants to see you again for a moment."

I went to him. When I entered the room, he turned his face to me and said, "I don't know it very well any more. What comes after the words Our Father?" I repeated the words for him, even the ones that say, "Your will be done." We prayed together.

A few days later he died. But of course, he did not die. Just as none of us will really die. We will pass over to our Father's house, and all the good we did will go with us, forever and ever.